CHESS FOR KIDS

This Book Belongs To:

_____

_____

_____

Table of Contents

Before you start reading, scan this QR Code to get all bonus content!

Introduction to Chess

1.1 Brief History and Origins of Chess

Hello, young chess enthusiasts! Are you ready to time travel? Let's set our time machine way back to start our chess journey.

Can you imagine a game so fascinating, so full of secrets and excitement, that people have been playing it for over a thousand years? Yes, you guessed right - that game is chess! While the exact origins of chess are shrouded in the mists of time, historians believe it began around the 6th century in a land far, far away known as India.

Back then, it wasn't exactly the game we know today. The game, called "chaturanga," which means "four divisions of the military" - infantry, cavalry, elephants, and chariotry - represented by pawn, knight, bishop, and rook. Can you imagine elephants and chariots on a chessboard? Sounds like a wild game, doesn't it?

As travelers journeyed from India to the Persian Empire, they took chaturanga with them, and Persians fell in love with it too! They called it "shatranj." The pieces started to look a little more like the ones we use today, but they still had some changes to go through.

Next stop on our time machine is Arabian land. When the Muslim people conquered Persia, they discovered this captivating game and helped spread it even further. It traveled all across the Muslim lands to North Africa and even to Europe.

In Europe, chess began to evolve into the game we know today. By the 15th century, during a time known as the Middle Ages, the rules were tweaked and modified. The queen became the most powerful piece on the board. Now, isn't that cool?

Fast forward to today, and chess has become a global game, played by millions of kids and adults alike, just like you! It's even called "The Game of Kings" because, for a long time, it was mostly played by nobles and royalty. But don't worry, you don't have to be a king or queen to play chess. All you need is a love for adventures and a keen mind ready to solve puzzles and create strategies. So, are you ready to make your move?

Let's go forward and dive into the exciting world of chess! Remember, every chess master was once a beginner who decided to make that first move. Your chess journey starts right here, right now!

1.2 Overview of the Game and its Objectives

Welcome back, chess explorers! Now that we've gone through our time machine journey, let's hop off and take a closer look at the game of chess. We'll unravel its mysteries and learn about its grand objective.

Do you know what a battlefield looks like? Well, a game of chess is like a friendly battlefield, but instead of fighting, we use our minds! That's right - chess is a game of strategy and tactics, almost like being a general leading an army.

The chessboard is your battlefield, and it's made up of 64 squares, half of them light (like the color of sunshine) and half of them dark (like the color of chocolate). These squares are laid out in an 8x8 grid - that's 8 squares down and 8 squares across.

On this battlefield, you have an army of 16 pieces: one king, one queen, two rooks, two knights, two bishops, and eight brave little pawns. Each of these pieces has a unique way of moving around the board, which we'll learn about later.

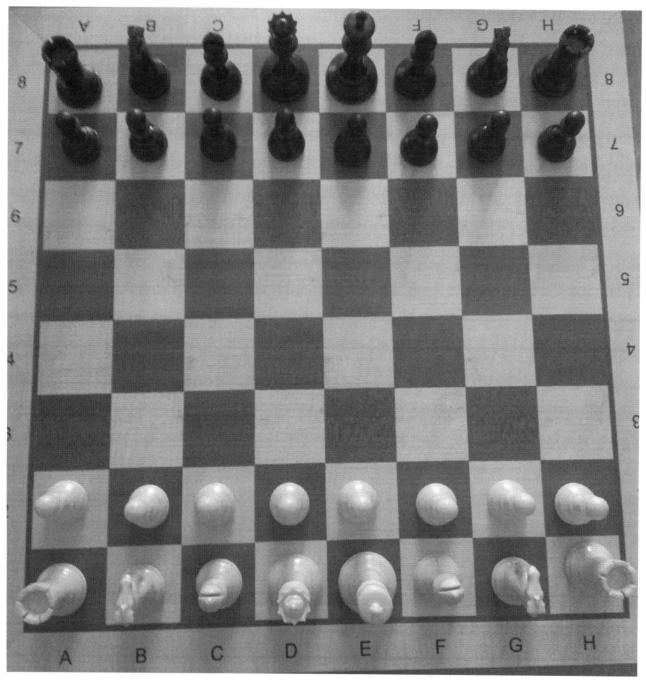

Now, let's talk about the main goal of the game. The king is the most important piece on the board. If he's trapped and cannot escape, we call that 'checkmate,' and the game is over. So, your mission, should you choose to accept it, is to protect your king while trying to checkmate your opponent's king.

It

sounds like a lot to take in, right? Don't worry! Remember, every master was once a beginner. So let's set out on this exciting journey together, step by step, and soon you'll be calling out 'checkmate' with a triumphant grin on your face!

Chapter 2: Chessboard and Pieces

2.1 Understanding the Chessboard and its Layout

Now that we know the origins of chess and the basics, it's time to dive deeper into the battlefield - the chessboard. In this chapter, we're going to dissect the chessboard, exploring its unique layout.

The Squares of the Chessboard

Imagine a kingdom where each piece of land is evenly divided into squares, forming a vast quilt that stretches as far as the eye can see. Welcome to the chessboard, a grid of 64 squares, neatly arranged in an 8x8 pattern. Can you picture that? Eight rows and eight columns, with each square just as important as the other.

This land is not uniform in color, though. It's a checkered field where half the squares are a warm, inviting light color, and the other half are a contrasting dark hue. Think of it like the days and nights of a month, alternating one after the other. There are 32 light-colored squares and 32 dark-colored ones. They all sit next to each other, creating a pattern that might remind you of a checkerboard or a patchwork quilt made from two different types of fabric.

Every square on this board is like a plot of land in our kingdom, a tiny territory where a piece can settle or pass through on its journey. Each square has a name, much like the way cities and towns have names. This helps the players know where their pieces are, and where they could move next. We'll delve deeper into the naming of these squares a little later on, but for now, just think of them as the places where all the action of our game will unfold.

Isn't it amazing that so much can happen on this simple grid of squares? Each square may be small on its own, but together, they form the battlefield where you'll lead your army of pieces into the captivating world of chess. So the next time you look at a chessboard, don't just see 64 squares. Instead, see a vibrant kingdom filled with opportunities for adventure, where every decision can bring victory one step closer.

Remember, the chessboard isn't just the playing field of the game; it's the canvas upon which you'll paint your strategies, your triumphs, and your story in the world of chess.

Ranks and Files

Now, let's dive a little deeper into the chessboard, our kingdom. Think of it not just as a collection of squares, but also as a perfectly organized grid. A city map that helps you navigate your chess pieces on their journey across the board.

Imagine that the chessboard is your kingdom and its squares are plots of land. But how do these pieces of land connect with each other? This is where our avenues, called 'files,' and our streets, known as 'ranks,' come into play. Just as you'd navigate a bustling city, these ranks and files help you move your chess pieces around the kingdom, from one square to another.

The chessboard is made up of eight rows stretching from top to bottom. These rows are what we call ranks. Think of these ranks like the rows of a cornfield or the lines on a sheet of lined paper. They run horizontally across the board, from one player's perspective to the other. In our kingdom, the ranks can be seen as the levels of terrain from the foot of a mountain up to the top.

On the other side, we have eight columns running from left to right. These are known as files and can be pictured as the vertical lines in a grid, like the columns of a Greek temple or a spreadsheet. In our kingdom's geography, the files are akin to long avenues that span the entire length of the city.

Now, why is it important to know about ranks and files? Well, they are like the compass of our chessboard kingdom, guiding the movement of the pieces. The files (columns) help your pieces to move up and down the board, while the ranks (rows) assist them to traverse left and right.

By mastering the layout of ranks and files, you are not just learning how to navigate the board, but also developing a strategic understanding of the game. Remember, in the world of chess, each square, each rank, and each file holds its strategic importance. So, while the game is played on the battlefield of 64 squares, it is won by those who can best navigate the avenues and streets of their chess kingdom.

Your Territory

Imagine, if you will, a wide river flowing majestically through the middle of your chessboard. It slices the board from top to bottom, dividing it into two equal halves. The side that you're seated on, the half of the board closest to you, becomes your territory. It's your very own kingdom, your realm within the larger world of the chessboard.

Think of this territory as your home base, the starting point for your army. Your chess pieces, the brave soldiers, start the game in this territory. They line up ready for battle, awaiting your orders. Picture it as a bustling fortress preparing for a grand adventure. It's your stronghold, your safe place. Remember, as the commanding general of your army, it is essential that you become intimately familiar with every nook and cranny of your territory.

Now, visualize your chess pieces placed in the territory. The Pawns are like the protective wall of your castle, standing tall and strong at the front, ready to march forward. Behind them, the other pieces are arrayed, your royalty, and your valiant Knights, ready to sally forth into the battlefield when the time is right. The King and Queen, positioned in the center of the back row, are the heart of your territory. They're like the king and queen of your chess kingdom, leading the charge from behind.

Just as a good ruler knows their kingdom, knowing your territory is critical in chess. Each square holds strategic importance and understanding this can often make the difference between victory and defeat. Take some time to get to know your territory, become familiar with the paths and potential strategies within your own half of the chessboard. Your understanding of your territory, your realm, will become your weapon as you lead your army into the wider battlefield, crossing that imaginary river into the opponent's side of the chessboard.

Remember, the chessboard is not just a game surface; it's a world. It's a kingdom waiting to be ruled. As you explore your territory, imagine the strategies you can create and the triumphs you can achieve. In chess, as in life, understanding your world is the key to conquering it.

Setting Up the Board Correctly

In chess, just like in many other things in life, starting right is crucial. When setting up the chessboard, the direction matters! You should place the board so that a light-

15

colored square is on your right-hand side. A simple phrase to remember is "white on the right," and you'll always start correctly.

Understanding the layout of the chessboard is the first step in becoming a great chess player. Think of yourself as a general looking at a map before a big battle. It's crucial to know every inch of your land and understand where every avenue leads.

2.2 Introduction to Chess Pieces

Now that we've journeyed through our kingdom's landscape, the chessboard, it's time to meet our most esteemed inhabitants, the chess pieces. Each piece has a distinct role and unique way of moving across the board.

2.2.1 The King

As we venture deeper into our chess kingdom, it's time to meet the most esteemed characters of all, the chess pieces. Each piece has its unique role in the game and carries a distinctive value. Let's start with the most crucial figure of all - the King.

<u>Appearance and Symbolism</u>

Take a look at your chess set, and you will find the King, the tallest piece on the board, wearing a crown with a cross at the top - a symbol of his royal status.

The King's crown is stately, often with intricate designs that vary depending on the chess set's style. The cross at the top of the crown signifies his rank above all other pieces. Some say the King's cross shows that he is both a warrior and a leader, ready to defend his kingdom to the very end.

Role on the Chessboard

In the game of chess, the King is the heart of the kingdom. He is the most vital piece on the chessboard. Your King's safety determines the fate of the game. If your King is trapped, a situation we call 'checkmate', the game is over. So protecting your King while planning to trap your opponent's King is the central goal of chess.

Yet, while the King's safety is paramount, he is not a weak figure hiding behind his subjects. The King is a decisive player in the endgame, capable of defending his territory and capturing opponent pieces.

Even though the King doesn't control the board like some of the other pieces we'll learn about, never underestimate his importance. In the game of chess, as in a real kingdom, without a King, there is no game.

The King's Special Ability: Castling

The King is also unique because he has a special ability called 'castling'. This is the only time in the game when more than one piece can move during a turn. In this exciting move, the King partners with a rook, his castle, to ensure his safety. But, like any special power, there are rules governing when and how the King can castle, which we'll learn about in a later chapter.

The King's role in chess is much more than just a royal figure to be protected. He's an active player with his own abilities.

2.2.2 The Queen

Appearance and Symbolism

Next, let's meet the most powerful piece on the chessboard, the Queen. She is a touch shorter than the King but don't let that fool you. She wears a crown, too, usually with more rounded or decorative points compared to the King's cross-topped crown.

In many ways, the Queen is like the King's advisor or general. She is the one who can swoop across the board, capturing enemies and defending her King. She's a symbol of power and flexibility, ready to take on any challenge that comes her way.

Role on the Chessboard

In the kingdom of chess, the Queen is the powerhouse. Unlike the King, whose main role is to stay safe, the Queen is the kingdom's active protector and a formidable attacker. She can control large areas of the board and is often the piece that your opponent fears the most.

But remember, with great power comes great responsibility! Losing your Queen can be a significant setback. So while you'll want to use her abilities to your advantage, you'll also need to think carefully about when and where to move her.

The Queen is a game changer. Using her effectively can often be the key to victory in your chess battles. But don't worry if you lose her, a smart and resourceful player can still turn the tide of battle without her.

And here's a fun fact: In the early versions of chess, the Queen wasn't as powerful. But during the Middle Ages, she was given the mighty powers she has now, in a rule change called the "Queen's leap." That certainly changed the game!

2.2.3 The Rook

Appearance and Symbolism

As we continue our journey across the chessboard, we next encounter the castle-like figures, the Rooks. With their sturdy towers and battlement crowns, they echo the might and strength of medieval castles.

The Rook symbolizes the walls of a castle, strong and impregnable. These pieces stand as defenders of the realm, guarding the King and the other pieces behind their unyielding fortifications.

Role on the Chessboard

On the chessboard, the Rooks are often the backbone of your defense and a significant part of your attacking force. They start the game in the corners of the board, like the towers in a castle. But as the game unfolds, they can take control of entire rows or columns, known as ranks and files in chess lingo.

Rooks have a unique quality. They are equally powerful in both the opening and the endgame stages. In the opening, they can connect with each other once your pieces have moved out into the battlefield. This connection, often referred to as "connecting the Rooks," is a sign of a well-developed position.

In the endgame, Rooks can be very potent due to their ability to swiftly move to action and reach any corner of the board. Also, they love open files or ranks where they can assert control and threaten the enemy.

Remember our discussion about the King's special move, Castling? Here's where the Rook plays his part. In castling, the Rook leaps over the King to provide an extra layer of protection and to bring itself into the game faster. This special ability is a crucial strategy you will learn to use effectively as you become more proficient in chess.

The strength of a Rook can sometimes be underestimated, especially by beginners, but as you progress in your chess journey, you'll find that the Rooks are indeed the silent powerhouses of the chessboard.

2.2.4 The Knight

Appearance and Symbolism

Continuing our tour across the chessboard, we next encounter the most unusual and recognizable pieces in the game, the Knights. They're easy to identify, as they're the ones shaped like a horse's head.

The Knight symbolizes the medieval horsemen, valiant and unpredictable. Its representation as a horse head harks back to the knights of old, brave warriors known for their courage and strategic prowess in the battlefield.

Role on the Chessboard

In the realm of chess, the Knight is the most unpredictable piece. Unlike other pieces that move in straight lines, the Knight leaps around the board in an 'L' shape. This unique movement allows the Knight to jump over other pieces, whether they're friend or foe, making it a tricky piece to deal with.

Knights are often the pieces that are brought into the game early. They're nimble, able to jump into the action quickly, and their unpredictable movement can sometimes catch an unsuspecting opponent off guard.

It's important to note, though, that while Knights are powerful in their unique way, they also have their limitations. Knights are "short-range" pieces, meaning they can't cross the board in a single move like the Rook or Queen. They often require more time and planning to maneuver into effective positions.

But despite these limitations, the Knight's unusual movement and jumping ability make it a tricky and valuable piece in your chess army. A well-positioned Knight can often be more powerful than a poorly positioned Rook or Queen!

2.2.5 The Bishop

Appearance and Symbolism

Continuing our journey on the chessboard, we now meet the Bishops, the spiritual leaders of our chess kingdom. You can recognize the Bishops by their tall, pointed hats, which are called miters and represent the traditional headgear of bishops in many cultures.

The Bishop piece is symbolic of wisdom and guidance, providing spiritual direction to the kingdom. Their presence on the chessboard adds a level of depth and complexity to the game, reflecting their role in offering strategic insights and counseling in real-world monarchies.

Role on the Chessboard

In the game of chess, the Bishops are long-range pieces that move diagonally across the board. This movement gives them the power to control the color of squares they stand on, either light or dark.

One of the most notable characteristics of the Bishops is their range. They can sprint across the chessboard in a single move, making them a significant force in both attack and defense. However, their limitation to only half the squares (of one color) on the board requires some strategic thinking for their effective use.

In the opening and middle game stages, Bishops are invaluable for controlling central squares from a distance. They are often developed early in the game to create threats and support other pieces. Bishops work well with Pawns and other pieces to create a powerful, interlocking network of control.

In the endgame, a pair of Bishops ("the Bishop pair") is often considered advantageous due to their ability to control both color complexes (light and dark squares), becoming a significant force to reckon with.

2.2.6 The Pawn

<u>**Appearance and Symbolism**</u>

We're now at the front lines of our chess kingdom where we find the Pawns, the humble yet indispensable members of our chess army. The Pawns are the smallest pieces on the board, easily recognized by their simplistic, rounded shape.

The Pawn symbolizes the foot soldiers, the commoners, or the serfs of a kingdom. While they may lack the authority or status of the other pieces, they're the foundation of the game, creating the structure on the chessboard and often deciding the fate of the other pieces.

Role on the Chessboard

In the game of chess, Pawns have a unique role. They're the only pieces that can't move backward, only forward, reflecting the foot soldiers' relentless march forward in a battlefield.

Pawns may seem insignificant due to their limited movement and lack of range compared to other pieces, but don't be fooled! They play a critical role in the game, often determining the structure of a position and the overall strategy of the play.

Your Pawns can form a strong defensive line, protecting your more valuable pieces. They can also become threats themselves, as a Pawn that reaches the other side of the board can be promoted, turning into any other piece you choose (except for a King).

Additionally, Pawns have a unique ability to capture differently than they move, taking opponent's pieces diagonally rather than straight forward. This ability often surprises new players and is something to keep in mind as you learn more about the game.

So, never underestimate the humble Pawns! With careful planning and strategic moves, these small but mighty pieces can turn the tide of a chess game.

Chapter 3: Basic Rules and Gameplay

3.1 The Concepts of Check, Checkmate, and Stalemate

It's now time to learn about some core concepts: check, checkmate, and stalemate. These terms might sound a little strange now, but they're as integral to the game of chess as touchdowns are to football or home runs are to baseball.

Check

"Check" is a term you'll encounter quite often on your chess journey. In fact, it is one of the most crucial words in the game. But what does it mean? What is its significance in the realm of chess? Well, to put it simply, "check" is the term we use when a player's King is under immediate threat of capture on the next move. It's a signal, a warning bell that your King is in danger and needs immediate attention.

Now, let's illustrate this concept. Imagine you're in the midst of a heated game. Your opponent's Queen, a powerhouse on the chessboard, has just moved and, in its new position, is directly attacking your King. In the language of chess, we say that your King is "in check." It's like a siren going off, a red flag signaling that your King is in danger. The game takes a pause here, with the word "check" reverberating in the air. Your King's safety has suddenly become the most pressing issue on the board.

When a King is in check, the game gives you a chance to respond. You cannot just proceed with your original plan as if nothing has happened. Your next move MUST be to address this threat. It's as if the rules of chess are saying, "Hold on! Your King is in danger. You need to take care of this first." There are three ways you can do so: you can move your King to a safe square, block the check with another piece, or capture the attacking piece. Each of these methods has its own nuances and strategic implications, which we'll explore more in later chapters.

However, it's essential to remember that being put in check isn't the end of the world, nor is it the end of the game. On the contrary, it's an integral part of the game that adds to the dynamic, strategic nature of chess. Each time your King is placed in check, it's a new puzzle to solve, a new challenge to overcome. It forces you to think, to strategize, and to consider the game from new angles. And remember, as you navigate the complexities of chess, dealing successfully with checks can lead you on the path to becoming a true chess champion.

Checkmate

If "check" is a caution, a red flag signaling immediate danger, then "checkmate" is the final siren, the endgame declaration. It's the climax of a chess battle, the point at which one player emerges victorious. To explain it in simple terms, "checkmate" is the term we use when a player's King is under attack (or in check), and there is no legal move that the player can make to remove the threat. This scenario marks the end of the game, with the opponent who delivered the checkmate declared the winner.

Picture this situation: You're in a gripping chess duel. The pieces have moved around, some have been traded, and now you find your King cornered. Your opponent's Queen, a versatile and powerful piece, along with a Rook, have teamed up and launched an attack on your King. They've created a situation where your King can't escape their threat, no matter where it moves. This is what we call "checkmate." It's as if your King has been caught in a trap, and there's no way out.

Checkmate isn't a situation that occurs randomly. It is the culmination of a series of strategic moves, a final blow that is meticulously planned and executed. Every move your opponent made, every piece they moved was leading up to this moment. The beauty of checkmate lies in its finality. It is not a mere threat like a check but the endpoint of the game, marking a clear victory for one player and defeat for the other.

However, it's important to remember that a checkmate is not a judgment of your skills as a chess player, but rather a signal to learn and improve. Experiencing a checkmate, whether you're on the delivering or receiving end, is an integral part of the game. It provides invaluable lessons on attack, defense, strategy, and planning. And remember, the goal of the game, the mission you're striving for, is to checkmate your opponent's King while protecting yours.

Stalemate

While the ultimate aim of chess is to corner the enemy King in a checkmate, there's another equally significant situation that can arise in the game: the "stalemate." The term might sound a little strange, but it describes a very specific situation in the game of chess. A stalemate is when a player is not in check, but has no legal move to make. Picture this - it's your turn, your King isn't under direct attack (or in check), but any move it makes will put it in check.

Imagine this scenario: Your King is isolated on one side of the board, and all the squares around it are under attack. Every lane of escape is blocked, and moving to any of them would place your King in check, which is not allowed in chess. You look around the board for another piece to move, but you find that there are no other pieces left or they are blocked and cannot move. This situation, where you cannot make a legal move but your King is not in check, is known as a "stalemate."

But here's the twist! In chess, a stalemate is considered a draw. That's right! The game ends there, and it's a tie, regardless of how many pieces each player has left on the board. It's almost like an unexpected plot twist in a story where the underdog suddenly finds a way out. So, even if you're down to your last King and your opponent has an army of pieces, you can still secure a draw if your opponent unwittingly forces a stalemate. Intriguing, isn't it?

Stalemate is a complex and fascinating element of chess that adds another layer of depth to the game. It's not merely about the pieces you have left, but how you use them. A player aiming for a checkmate might inadvertently cause a stalemate, changing the outcome of the game completely. Therefore, it's essential to not only plan your attacks but also to anticipate your opponent's moves and possible escape routes.

Understanding check, checkmate, and stalemate is a critical step in becoming a chess player. It's the crux of your journey—the target you're aiming for, and the pitfall you're trying to avoid. As you play and gain more experience, you'll become more comfortable with these concepts and how to navigate them in your games.

Now that we've learned about these important concepts, we're ready to understand how the chess game starts and ends. Stay tuned!

3.2 How to Start and End a Game

We've already uncovered some key concepts such as check, checkmate, and stalemate. Now, it's time to actually start our chess journey – by learning how to properly set up a game and understanding how a game ends.

Setting Up the Chessboard

Before we engage in any epic chess battles, we need to make sure our battlefield, the chessboard, is set up correctly. As simple as it may seem, a proper setup is the first fundamental step in playing a proper game of chess.

- Position the board: Begin by placing the chessboard between the two players. An essential rule to remember is that the lower-right corner square should always be a light-colored square, often referred to as "white on the right."

https://www.shutterstock.com/fr/image-photo/classic-empty-chessboard-on-brown-wooden-1927489550

- Place the rooks: The Rooks are your castle towers, and they belong on the corners of your board. So, let's put them in their places!
- Place the knights: Knights, the horse-headed pieces, are positioned right next to the Rooks. They're the agile protectors of your kingdom.
- Place the bishops: Your Bishops, the pieces with a tall, pointed top, come next. They stand right next to the Knights, ready to leap diagonally across the board.
- Place the royalty: The Queen and the King are the royalty of your chess kingdom. The Queen goes on the remaining square of her color (remember, the Queen "dresses to match"), and the King takes the remaining square.
- Set up the pawns: Last but not least, set up your row of Pawns in front of your other pieces. These brave soldiers form the first line of defense of your kingdom.

After both players set up their pieces, the board is ready. Every piece is in its place, eagerly waiting to participate in the forthcoming strategic battle.

Starting the Game

Once our battlefield, the chessboard, is perfectly set up, it's time to bring our chess pieces to life and kickstart the adventure! In the grand game of chess, tradition dictates that the player commanding the white pieces gets the privilege to make the first move. You can decide who gets the white pieces by a simple coin toss, drawing straws, or any other method that you find fair and exciting.

The Importance of the First Move

The power of the first move cannot be understated. You see, making the first move gives the white player an initial advantage, or what chess enthusiasts call "the initiative." Having the initiative means you're the one making threats that your opponent must respond to. This can be a powerful position if used correctly, as it allows the white player to dictate the tempo of the game early on.

The Opening Phase

Once the first move has been made, both players enter into what is known as the 'opening' phase of the game. The opening phase comprises the initial series of moves where players set their pieces in motion and start laying out their strategies. This phase can significantly influence the trajectory of the entire game.

The opening moves are essential for a few reasons. Firstly, they help control the center of the board, which provides your pieces with more mobility and options to attack or defend. Secondly, the opening moves help in the development of your pieces, particularly the Knights and Bishops, setting them on powerful squares from where they can control the board. Lastly, the opening phase is where you aim to ensure the safety of your King, usually by a move called 'castling' that we will explore in later chapters.

Strategies for the Opening Phase

During the opening phase, a golden rule to remember is - control the center, develop your pieces, and ensure your King's safety. The center of the chessboard is a prime piece of real estate. Controlling the center squares gives your pieces the freedom to move around the board more efficiently. It allows them to swing from one side to the other, ready to jump into the action wherever they are needed.

Developing your pieces, especially Knights and Bishops, is equally crucial during the opening phase. Knights and Bishops are faster to get into the game than the Queen and Rooks, and moving them towards the center of the board can exert pressure on your opponent early on. The King, although powerful, is vulnerable. Hence, it's usually wise to tuck your King away safely by castling.

The strategies for the opening phase might seem a lot to digest right now, but don't worry! As we move forward in our chess journey, we will break down these concepts in detail, helping you to grasp these strategies and apply them in your games. For now, remember, every great chess player was once a beginner, just like you.

Ending the Game

Chess, despite its almost infinite complexities, eventually draws to a close, concluding the tense mental duel between the two players. The curtain falls on a chess game primarily in one of three ways: checkmate, stalemate, or by agreement between the players. Let's delve deeper into each of these terms, unraveling their meanings and how they shape the outcome of a chess game.

Checkmate

The checkmate is the grand finale that every chess player aspires to deliver. When a player's King is in check — meaning, it's under attack — and there's no legal move that removes the threat, it's a checkmate. A checkmate signifies that the King is trapped with no means of escape. It's like being caught in a spider's web, with the spider inching closer and there's no way out. The player who manages to weave this intricate web and trap their opponent's King is the triumphant victor.

However, achieving a checkmate isn't easy. It requires careful planning, strategic maneuvering of pieces, and, most importantly, a keen understanding of your opponent's plans. Many games of chess are a tussle between the players, each attempting to trap the other's King while defending their own. The player who can juggle attack and defense more effectively often emerges victorious with a well-deserved checkmate.

Stalemate

Stalemate, on the other hand, is like a thrilling movie ending with an unexpected twist. If it's a player's turn, and they can't make a legal move, but their King isn't in check, the game ends in a stalemate, and it's a draw. This means that even though the King isn't under direct attack, it can't move without walking into a threat, and none of the other pieces can move. It's like being stuck in a traffic jam with no way to move forward or backward, even though your home is just around the corner!

Stalemate often comes into play in the endgame, where fewer pieces on the board sometimes lead to these complex situations. While a stalemate doesn't provide the triumphant feeling of a checkmate, it's still an interesting part of the game that brings its own set of challenges. Understanding and foreseeing stalemate situations can sometimes save you from the brink of defeat!

Agreement between Players

Finally, a chess game can also conclude by mutual agreement between the players. Sometimes, the battlefield reaches a state where neither player has a clear path to victory, or it becomes apparent that the game is inexorably heading towards a stalemate. In such scenarios, both players may agree to call it a draw.

Drawing by agreement can occur at any stage of the game, although it is more common in the middle and endgame stages. Mutual respect and a shared understanding of the game's complexities often lead to these agreed draws. Even though these games don't end with the dramatic flair of a checkmate or stalemate, they represent the intellectual depth of chess where players recognize an evenly-matched situation.

In the end, whether through a stunning checkmate, a cunning stalemate, or an agreed draw, every game of chess provides a learning opportunity.

Now, equipped with this knowledge, you're all set to begin your chess games and experiment with the thrilling combinations this game has to offer.

Chapter 4: Piece Movements and Capturing

4.1 Detailed Explanations of How Each Chess Piece Moves

4.1.1 The King

The King, the most vital piece in the game of chess, commands respect due to the very importance of its survival. A game of chess is essentially a battle to protect your King while threatening your opponent's. As we have already understood, losing the King to a checkmate means losing the game. Therefore, knowing how the King moves is crucial to both attack and defense in chess.

King's Movement

The King can move one square in any direction: vertically, horizontally, or diagonally. Imagine the King at the center of a 3x3 grid. The King can move to any of the eight squares surrounding it, as long as the move is legal. The term 'legal,' in this context, means that the King cannot move to a square under attack by an enemy piece.

The King's Power

Though the King's movement seems limited compared to some other pieces, never underestimate its power. In the endgame, when fewer pieces are on the board, the King can prove quite powerful. It can become an aggressive piece, helping to corner the enemy King or support its own pawns to reach the other side of the board and become Queens!

Special Move: Castling

The King also has a special move called 'castling,' which is the only move that allows two pieces, the King and a Rook, to move at once. Castling is a crucial move that serves two purposes: It allows the King to move to a safer position and connects the Rooks, increasing their power. We will discuss castling in a separate chapter as it requires a detailed explanation due to its unique nature.

Remember, the King's safety should be your utmost priority in a game of chess. The King isn't just a piece on the chessboard; it's your main hero. The fate of your game rests in its hands - or rather, on its moves!

Next, let's move on to understanding the movements of other chess pieces and appreciate their unique roles in this grand game.

4.1.2 The Queen

The Queen is the most powerful piece on the chessboard. She is the commander of the army, the force that instills fear in the opponent. While the King provides the game's objective, the Queen brings versatility and strength. Her wide range of movements makes her a key player in both attack and defense.

Queen's Movement

The Queen is the powerhouse of chess because she can move any number of squares along a rank, file, or diagonal. That means she can move horizontally, vertically, or diagonally across the board. This is a combination of the powers of a Rook and a Bishop. Thus, the Queen has the freedom to control the board if she's positioned wisely and is unobstructed.

The Queen's Might

The Queen's strength comes from her ability to control the battlefield from a distance. Her long-range attacks can disrupt the opponent's plans and can often lead to early wins if the opponent is unprepared. However, remember that losing your Queen early in the game can put you at a significant disadvantage. So, while she is a strong piece, she also needs protection.

Versatility is Key

Versatility is the Queen's biggest asset. She can switch from one side of the board to the other in a single move, pressurize multiple pieces at once, and get out of danger swiftly. Therefore, utilizing your Queen effectively can often make the difference between victory and defeat.

Learning how to use the Queen effectively is a significant step in mastering chess. But always remember, with great power comes great responsibility. Make sure to keep your Queen safe while using her powers to control the game. Now, let's move on to understand the movements of the other unique chess pieces.

4.1.3 The Rook

The Rook, represented by a castle or a tower, is one of the heavy artillery pieces in your chess army. Though not as versatile as the Queen, the Rook's strength and range of motion make it a critical piece in your strategies, especially in the later stages of the game.

Rook's Movement

The Rook can move any number of squares along a rank or file. This means it can move horizontally or vertically across the board. No jumping over other pieces is allowed for the Rook. If an enemy piece lies in its path, the Rook can capture it by moving to its square and then stopping.

The Rook's Role

Rooks are particularly powerful pieces when they are protecting each other and working in tandem. This is often referred to as "connecting the Rooks." When placed on the same rank or file, the Rooks can control significant space on the board and are often key players in delivering checkmate.

Special Move: Castling

Like the King, the Rook also participates in a special move called 'castling.' This move enhances the Rook's mobility, and it's the only instance when the Rook can move over another piece. It's a vital strategy for getting the Rook into the game while safeguarding the King. More details about castling will be explained in a separate chapter.

Mastering the use of the Rook can give you a significant advantage, particularly in the endgame where Rooks can control many squares and exert pressure on the opponent. The Rook, with its straightforward yet powerful moves, brings a unique dimension to the intricate game of chess. Let's proceed to understand the movements of other chess pieces and discover the roles they play in this beautiful game.

4.1.4 The Knight

Ah, the Knight! It is indeed a unique piece in the game of chess. Unlike other pieces that move in straight lines, the Knight leaps over other pieces in an L-shaped pattern. This ability to jump over other pieces, combined with its unique movement, often makes the Knight a tricky and unpredictable piece to handle.

Knight's Movement

Each move of the Knight consists of two parts: it first moves two squares along a rank or file, like a Rook, and then makes one more move at a right angle, like stepping to the side. To put it simply, the Knight's move is like an "L." It's important to note that the Knight is the only piece that can 'jump' over other pieces.

The Knight's Unpredictability

Because the Knight can jump over other pieces, it remains unaffected by obstacles in its path. This characteristic makes the Knight exceptionally agile and unpredictable, capable of fork attacks, where it can attack two pieces simultaneously.

These fork attacks can often turn the tide in a game, making the Knight a piece to be handled with caution.

The Knight's ability to disrupt the opponent's plans, combined with its unique movement pattern, makes it a valuable player in the game of chess. Knowing how to use your Knights effectively will bring an extra layer of depth and strategy to your game. Now, let's move on to learn about the movements and roles of the remaining chess pieces.

4.1.5 The Bishop

The Bishop, a piece that sits next to the King and Queen at the start of the game, is a long-range operator with a unique method of movement. While its scope might seem limited at first glance, the Bishop is actually a powerful piece capable of controlling the board from corner to corner.

<u>Bishop's Movement</u>

The Bishop can move any number of squares diagonally. This means that it stays on the same color square for the entire game. If it starts on a white square, it will always be on a white square, and if it starts on a black square, it will always stay on a black square. This is why each player has one Bishop for the game's white squares and one Bishop for the game's black squares.

The Bishop's Range

While the Bishop might be confined to a particular color, this does not limit its power. The Bishop can control long diagonals and can often surprise the opponent by exerting pressure from far corners of the board. When the Bishops work together, they can control a large number of squares and can be formidable forces on the board.

The Bishop, with its diagonal movement and long-range capability, brings a distinct dynamic to the game of chess. Its ability to slide across the board, covering great distances, can play a crucial role in both defense and offense. Understanding the Bishop's power and using it strategically can help you control the game effectively. As we continue to explore the movement of the remaining chess pieces, you will begin to see the beautiful complexity of chess.

4.1.6 The Pawn

The Pawn, the smallest piece in chess, often surprises with its unique and multifaceted capabilities. The Pawns, despite their humble appearance, hold the game together and play a critical role in the battlefield of chess.

Pawn's Movement

Pawns move differently from all other pieces. Normally, a Pawn moves forward exactly one square. However, the first time you move each Pawn, it has the option to move forward two squares. Remember, Pawns cannot move backward or sideways - they always move straight ahead.

Pawn's Capture

Now, here's where things get interesting. Pawns capture differently than they move. They capture diagonally, one square forward to the left or right. This unique method of capture often comes as a surprise to new players.

Special Moves: En Passant and Promotion

Pawns are also involved in two special chess rules. The first one is "en passant," which is a special pawn capturing move, and the other one is "promotion," which allows a Pawn that reaches the other side of the board to become any other chess piece (except a King). These special rules add more depth to the humble Pawn, and we'll discuss them in a separate chapter.

The Pawn, despite being the smallest piece, brings an exceptional depth to the game. Its distinctive movement and capture method, coupled with the special moves of "en passant" and "promotion," create strategic richness that makes chess a game of unlimited possibilities. As we venture further, you'll continue to see how each piece's movements contribute to the overall strategy of the game.

48

4.2 Strategies for Capturing Opponent's Pieces

4.2.1 Capturing the King

In the game of chess, the ultimate goal is not exactly to 'capture' the opponent's King, but rather to place it in a position where it is threatened with capture, and there's no legal move left to remove that threat. This situation is called "checkmate." However, the journey towards achieving checkmate involves smart maneuvers and capturing other pieces to clear your path towards the enemy King. Let's dive into some strategies that can be used to corner the opponent's King.

The Value of Checks

A "check" is a situation where the King is under threat of capture in the next move. Putting your opponent's King in check forces them to react immediately and can disrupt their overall game strategy. While delivering random checks without a clear strategy won't help much, a well-planned series of checks can corner the opponent's King and lead to checkmate.

Removing the Defenders

Just as in a real battlefield, the King in a chess game is usually well guarded by other pieces known as "defenders." These pieces (like Pawns, Knights, Bishops, and even the Queen) surround the King and try to protect it from attacks. Strategically capturing these defenders is an effective way to expose the opponent's King and set up for checkmate.

51

Forcing the King to Move

In many cases, forcing the opponent's King to move can lead to a favorable position. You can achieve this by using tactics such as forks, pins, and skewers, where you threaten more than one piece or square at a time. These strategies can be complicated for beginners, but we'll cover them in more detail in later chapters.

Remember, the King is the most important piece in the game of chess. Your ultimate goal is to trap the opponent's King in a checkmate situation while protecting your own King. The strategies to do so can be complex, but with practice and understanding of the game's rules and pieces, you'll be able to plot your path towards checkmate effectively. As we move on to discuss strategies for capturing other pieces, you'll develop a richer understanding of the game's complexity.

54

4.2.2 Capturing the Queen

The Queen, being the most powerful piece on the chessboard, is a valuable target. Her wide range of movement and capability to control large sections of the board make her a formidable opponent. Here are some strategies to consider when aiming to capture your opponent's Queen.

Exposing the Queen

Often, players use their Queen aggressively in the early game to put pressure on the opponent. This, however, can expose the Queen to threats. Look for opportunities where your opponent's Queen might have ventured too far without enough protection.

Trapping the Queen

The Queen is extremely valuable, so a player will typically move their Queen to avoid capture if it's threatened. However, by controlling key squares around the Queen, it's possible to limit its movement and trap it.

Exchange and Sacrifice

In certain situations, it might be worthwhile to sacrifice a less valuable piece (like a Bishop or Knight) to capture the opponent's Queen. This tactic is also known as an "exchange," and it's a common strategy used to gain an advantage.

Remember, while capturing your opponent's Queen can provide a significant advantage, it's essential not to tunnel vision on this strategy. Chess is a complex game that requires a broad view of the entire board and careful consideration of all the pieces in play. As we continue discussing strategies for capturing other pieces, you'll see how each piece's unique capabilities contribute to the overall strategy of the game.

4.2.3 Capturing the Rook

The Rooks are valuable pieces in the game of chess due to their ability to control both rows and columns from any position on the board. A player who can capture their opponent's Rooks while keeping theirs has a considerable advantage. Let's go over some strategies that can help you capture your opponent's Rooks.

Pin the Rook

A common way to threaten a Rook is to "pin" it to the King or Queen. In a pin, the Rook is stuck protecting a more valuable piece and can't move without exposing that piece to capture.

Trap the Rook

Just like the Queen, Rooks can be trapped if they're not careful about where they move. The Rook needs open spaces to be effective, and if the board is crowded with pieces, it can become vulnerable to being trapped.

Exploit the Back Rank

Rooks often stay on the back rank (the first row of squares for White, the last row for Black) at the beginning of the game. If your opponent's back rank is poorly defended, you might be able to launch a successful attack that targets their Rook.

Remember, the goal of chess isn't just about capturing pieces but about controlling the board and positioning your pieces advantageously. While capturing your opponent's Rooks can be beneficial, it's equally important to protect your own and use them effectively. As we delve further into capturing strategies, keep in mind the importance of each piece and the role it plays in the grand game of chess.

61

4.2.4 Capturing the Knight

Knights are unique pieces in chess because they're the only pieces that can "jump" over other pieces. Their distinctive L-shaped move can surprise the unwary opponent, making them powerful in certain situations. Here are some strategies to consider when targeting your opponent's Knights.

Restrict the Knight's Movement

Knights are most powerful when they're positioned near the center of the board because they can reach more squares from there. By controlling the center and limiting the Knight's access, you can restrict its effectiveness.

Target Unprotected Knights

Like any piece, a Knight is vulnerable if left unprotected. Always be on the lookout for opportunities to capture Knights that have ventured too far from their other pieces.

Forking a Knight

Because Knights have a unique movement pattern, they can sometimes be vulnerable to forks, where one of your pieces attacks two of the opponent's pieces at the same time. With careful planning, you can force your opponent to make difficult decisions about which piece to save.

Capturing Knights can help eliminate threats and give you an advantage, but always remember that the goal is to checkmate your opponent's King. Keep this endgame in mind as you plan your strategies and make your moves. As we continue to explore different pieces and strategies, you'll see how these lessons can be applied to create a well-rounded game strategy.

4.2.5 Capturing the Bishop

The Bishops, with their diagonal movement, are crucial for controlling the board's color complexes. Having both Bishops can be a significant advantage since they can control both light and dark squares. Here are a few strategies to consider when trying to capture your opponent's Bishops.

Target Unprotected Bishops

Like all pieces, a Bishop is vulnerable if it is unprotected and within the range of your pieces. Watch out for opportunities where a Bishop has been left unguarded and you can safely capture it.

Trap the Bishop

Bishops require open diagonals to be effective. If the game board becomes crowded or blocked, a Bishop can quickly become trapped. Look for opportunities where you can limit the Bishop's mobility and trap it.

Forking a Bishop

Just like the Knight, a Bishop can be targeted with a fork, where one of your pieces simultaneously threatens two of the opponent's pieces. If you spot a potential fork that could involve a Bishop, it might be worth pursuing.

Capturing Bishops can help in controlling the board's color complexes and reducing threats from your opponent. However, the overall goal is to achieve checkmate, so always consider your broader game strategy as you make your moves. As we explore further strategies and pieces, you'll get a more profound understanding of the many different paths to victory in chess.

4.2.6 Capturing the Pawn

Pawns may be the smallest pieces on the chessboard, but they play a vital role in the game of chess. They form the "skeleton" of your position, controlling key squares and supporting your more powerful pieces. Here are a few strategies to capture your opponent's Pawns.

Target Isolated and Backward Pawns

Isolated Pawns (those that have no neighboring Pawns on adjacent files) and backward Pawns (those that are behind their neighbors and can't be defended by other Pawns) are often easy targets. They can't be protected by other Pawns, so they're vulnerable to attacks from your pieces.

Capture "En Passant"

This is a special pawn capturing move in chess. If a pawn moves two squares from its starting position and lands beside an opponent's pawn, that opponent has the option to capture the first pawn "en passant" as if it had only moved one square forward.

Pawn Chains and Breaks

Pawn chains are groups of pawns of the same color that defend each other on adjacent diagonal squares. These structures can be powerful, but they can also be vulnerable at their base. Look for opportunities to attack the base of your opponent's Pawn chain to try to break it apart.

Remember, Pawns have a unique role in chess. Not only can they capture opposing pieces and help control the board, but they can also be promoted if they reach the opposite side of the board. As we move forward, you'll see how to leverage the dual nature of the humble Pawn, from foot soldier to a potential queen!

Chapter 5: Opening Principles and Strategies

5.1 Introduction to Common Opening Principles

Chess is a game that requires strategic thinking right from the start, and the opening moves of a game can set the stage for everything that follows. Here are some basic principles you should keep in mind when making your opening moves.

Control the Center

The center of the chessboard, especially the squares e4, e5, d4, and d5, is the most critical area to control. Pieces placed in the center have a broader range of movement and can reach more parts of the board.

Develop Your Pieces

In the opening, you should aim to move your Knights and Bishops to good squares where they control the center and have options for future moves. As a general rule, try to move each piece only once in the opening to get as many pieces into play as possible.

Protect Your King

The King is your most valuable piece, so its safety is paramount. Try to castle early in the game, which moves your King to a safer location and also connects your Rooks.

E　　F　　G　　H

Don't Make Unnecessary Pawn Moves

While Pawns play a critical role in chess, moving them too much in the opening can leave your pieces underdeveloped. Focus on using your Pawns to control the center and open lines for your pieces.

Avoid Premature Attacks

In the opening, your primary focus should be on controlling the center and piece development. A premature attack, especially before your pieces are well-developed, can leave your position vulnerable.

Remember, the opening is all about setting up your game for success. By following these basic principles, you can build a solid foundation that prepares you for the middle and endgame. Now, let's see how to use these principles to create effective opening strategies!

5.2 Strategies for Controlling the Center of the Board

Controlling the center is one of the most critical aspects of the opening in chess. The player who controls the center has more room for their pieces to move and can more easily attack the opponent's pieces. Here are some strategies to help you gain control of the center early in your games.

Use Your Pawns Wisely

One of the most straightforward strategies to control the center is to move your e-pawn or d-pawn 2 squares forward on your first move. This not only opens up lines for your Bishop and Queen but also starts your control of the center.

Develop Your Knights and Bishops

Knights and Bishops are often the first pieces you should develop because they can control the center without being vulnerable. The knights are usually developed to the squares f3 and c3 (for white) or f6 and c6 (for black). The bishops can be developed to squares that do not block your own pawns and control the center.

Don't Overextend

While it's essential to control the center, it's also crucial not to overextend. Overextension occurs when you push your pawns too far into the center early in the game, leaving them undefended.

Counter Your Opponent's Moves

If your opponent is attempting to control the center, look for ways to counter their moves. This could involve using your pawns to challenge their central pawns or using your pieces to attack their central pieces.

Remember, controlling the center is about balance. You want to position your pieces and pawns to exert control, but you also need to keep them defended and avoid overextending. By mastering this balance, you'll be off to a great start in your games. Now let's look at how these opening strategies can come into play in the middle game.

Chapter 6: Middle Game Tactics

6.1 Tactical Concepts like Forks, Pins, and Skewers

Once you've established your opening and have control over the board, it's time to head into the heart of the game - the middle game. This is where the real fun starts! Chess isn't just about the pieces you have, but how you use them. By understanding and utilizing certain tactical concepts, you can take control of the game. Let's explore some of these tactics: forks, pins, and skewers.

Forks

A fork in chess is a tactic where a single piece makes two or more direct attacks at once. Essentially, your piece threatens two of your opponent's pieces simultaneously. That's like being a superhero with the power to be in two places at once! Usually, it's the Knights who are the champions of forking because of their unique ability to jump over other pieces.

Pins

A pin is a situation in chess where an opponent's piece is threatened and cannot move without exposing a more valuable piece. It's like your opponent's piece is stuck to the board with a giant pin! Bishops, Rooks, and Queens are great at creating pins because they can control long diagonals and straight lines on the board.

Skewers

A skewer is a bit like a reverse pin. In a skewer, a valuable piece is attacked and must move to avoid capture, but in doing so, it exposes another piece which can then be captured. It's like when you skewer vegetables and meat on a kebab stick; you have to eat the first piece to get to the next one. Like pins, skewers work best with Bishops, Rooks, and Queens, because of their long-range.

Understanding these tactics can make you a much stronger player. Practice them and soon you'll be spotting opportunities for forks, pins, and skewers all over the board. Up next, we'll discuss strategies for attacking and defending in the middle game. Stay tuned!

6.2 Strategies for Attacking and Defending Pieces

The middle game in chess is where battles truly begin. It's like a puzzle that needs to be solved, and the player who can better identify the opportunities to attack, while also defending their pieces, is the one who usually gets the upper hand. Let's take a closer look at some strategies to help you navigate these waters.

<u>Attacking Strategies</u>

Spotting Weaknesses

Look for any undefended or poorly defended pieces in your opponent's position. These pieces are ripe targets for your attacks! Remember our superhero Knight who could fork two pieces at once? He loves finding undefended pieces to attack.

Creating Threats

A good attack often involves creating multiple threats simultaneously. This is also known as a "double attack". When you attack two pieces at once, your opponent can only respond to one threat, leaving you to capture the other piece.

Defending Strategies

Value Your Pieces

Remember that each of your pieces has a value, and you should try to protect your more valuable pieces (Queen, Rooks) from attacks. This might involve moving a threatened piece to a safer square or protecting it with another piece.

King Safety

Your King is the most important piece on the board. If he is captured, it's game over! It's essential to keep your King safe, often by castling early in the game and avoiding unnecessary risks with your King's safety.

Important thing to remember: chess is a game of balance. You have to weigh up when to launch an attack and when to focus on defending. Keep practicing these strategies, and soon you'll start seeing improvements in your middle game!

Chapter 7: Endgame Techniques

7.1 Basic Endgame Principles and Strategies

You've navigated the waters of the opening and middle game, and now it's time to bring your ship home safely. Welcome to the endgame! This is when there are few pieces left on the board and the Kings come out to play. It might seem simpler with fewer pieces, but the endgame is a test of strategy and foresight. Let's learn some basic principles and strategies to guide you.

King Activation

In the opening and middle game, the King usually stays safe behind the army of other pieces. But in the endgame, the King transforms from a timid leader into a brave warrior. The King becomes a very strong piece that can help you attack and defend.

Pawn Structure

Pawns, the humble foot soldiers, become very important in the endgame. Your goal should be to create a "passed pawn"—a pawn that no enemy pawns can stop from promoting to a Queen.

The Principle of Two Weaknesses

In the endgame, creating two threats (or weaknesses) that your opponent has to deal with simultaneously can often lead to victory. While your opponent is busy handling one issue, you can make progress with the other.

Zugzwang

Zugzwang is a German word meaning "compulsion to move." In chess, it refers to a situation where any move a player makes will weaken their position. If you can maneuver your opponent into a zugzwang, you can often force them to make a mistake.

Mastering the endgame takes patience and practice. But remember, every grandmaster was once a beginner, and they all had to learn these strategies just like you. So, keep practicing, and soon you'll become an expert at navigating the endgame. On to the next chapter where we'll learn about checkmating patterns and techniques!

7.2 Understanding Checkmating Patterns and Techniques

Ahh, the sweet taste of victory! Nothing in chess is more satisfying than delivering a checkmate to your opponent. In this section, we'll uncover some common checkmating patterns and techniques that can help you end the game with a bang. So, let's get started!

The Back Rank Checkmate

The back rank checkmate is a common pattern, especially among beginners. This happens when a Rook or Queen traps the opponent's King on the back rank (the first or eighth rank), and it's blocked by its own pieces.

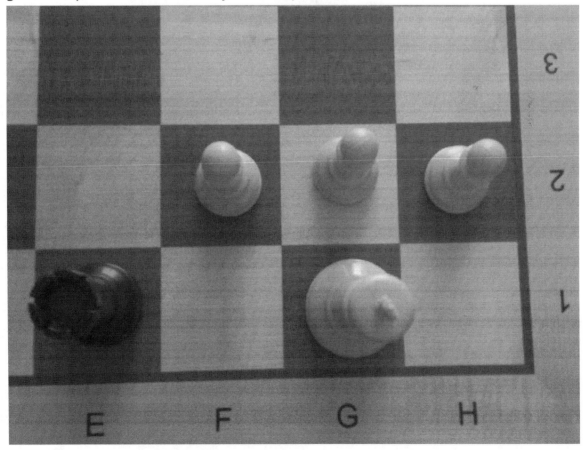

The Smothered Checkmate

This is a checkmate that happens when a King is all surrounded (smothered) by its own pieces, and a brave Knight delivers the final blow. The King has nowhere to run and is checkmated by the enemy Knight!

The Fool's Mate

The Fool's Mate is the quickest checkmate possible in a game of chess. It happens when a player carelessly exposes their King in the opening moves and the opponent's Queen delivers a swift checkmate.

The Scholar's Mate

The Scholar's Mate is another quick checkmate that can occur if a player isn't careful in the opening. In this scenario, the Queen and a Bishop team up to corner the opposing King.

These checkmate patterns are tools in your chess toolbox. Knowing them helps you to avoid falling into these traps and to seize the opportunity when your opponent slips. Like any tool, the key is to know when to use them. Keep practicing, and you'll develop an instinct for recognizing these patterns. Now that we've conquered checkmating patterns and techniques, we'll move on to the exciting world of chess notation in our next chapter!

Chapter 8: Chess Puzzles and Exercises

8.1 Solving Chess Puzzles to Improve Tactical Skills

Have you ever solved a jigsaw puzzle? Finding the right piece and fitting it into the correct place can be satisfying, right? Chess puzzles aren't very different. They're like brainy jigsaw puzzles where you need to find the best move or series of moves. Solving chess puzzles can greatly improve your tactical skills, making you a stronger player.

Why Chess Puzzles?

Chess puzzles help improve:

- Tactical Vision: These puzzles teach you to spot opportunities for checks, captures, and threats.

- Calculation Skills: They enhance your ability to think ahead and calculate multiple moves in advance.

- Familiarity with Patterns: Puzzles are great for learning common tactical patterns like forks, pins, and skewers.

How to Solve Chess Puzzles?

Chess puzzles usually involve a specific board setup, and your task is to find the best move or sequence of moves. Here's a step-by-step guide to solving them:

1. Study the Board: Look at all the pieces on the board, both yours and your opponent's.
2. Identify Threats and Opportunities: Are any pieces threatened? Can any be captured?
3. Visualize Moves: Try to visualize the moves in your head. Remember, a move may involve your pieces or your opponent's.
4. Solve the Puzzle: Once you think you have the solution, make the moves on the board.

Practice Chess Puzzles

Now, it's time for you to practice! Remember, the more puzzles you solve, the better you'll become at seeing important tactics during your games. You can find puzzles in chess books, websites, and even some chess-playing apps.

8.2 Interactive Exercises to Reinforce Chess Concepts

Learning chess is a bit like learning to play a musical instrument or a new language. Practicing regularly can help you become better and more comfortable.

Interactive exercises provide this practice in an engaging and fun way. Here are a few exercises you can try:

Exercise 1: Piece Movement

The objective of this exercise is to reinforce your understanding of how each piece moves and captures.

- Setup: Place a single piece (say, a Knight) on the board.
- Task: Move the Knight across every square of the board without landing on the same square twice.
- Tips: Remember, the Knight is the only piece that can jump over other pieces!

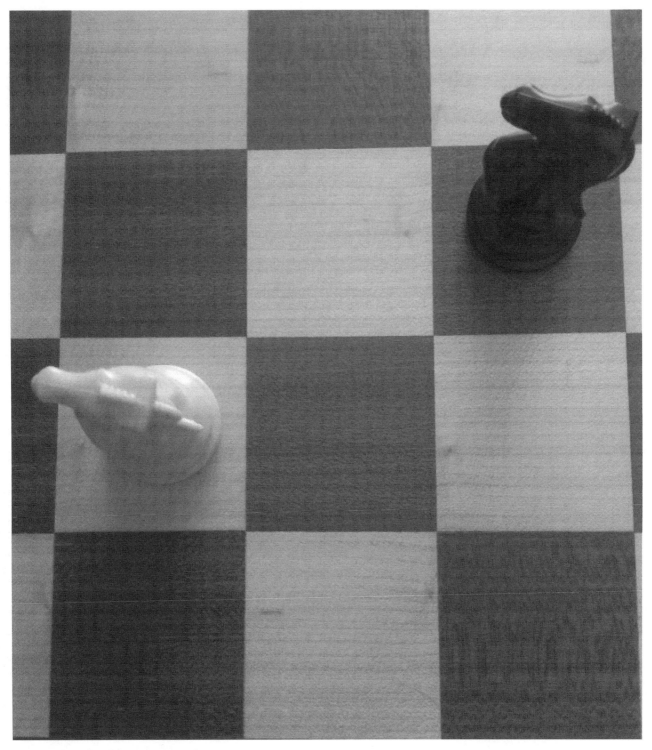

Exercise 2: The Pawn Game

This game will help you understand how Pawns move and capture, and it introduces the concept of promoting a Pawn to a Queen.

- Setup: Clear all pieces from the board except for the Pawns.
- Task: The goal is to reach your opponent's back rank with one of your Pawns.
- Rules: Remember, Pawns capture diagonally and cannot move backward!

Exercise 3: Pin the Tail on the Donkey

This fun exercise helps you practice the chess tactic known as "pinning."

- Setup: Set up the board so that one of your Bishops can pin an opponent's Knight to their Queen.
- Task: Try to pin the Knight to the Queen, making sure the Knight can't move without exposing the Queen to capture.
- Hint: This exercise will require you to think a few moves ahead!

Exercise 4: The Checkmate Drill

The objective of this exercise is to practice delivering a checkmate.

- Setup: Set up a board with a King and a Queen against a lone King.
- Task: Try to checkmate the opposing King using your King and Queen.
- Hint: Your King and Queen should work together like partners in a dance, controlling the opposing King's movements.

CONCLUSION

As we conclude this delightful journey into the world of chess, we look back and see the vast landscape we've traversed. From the simple setup of the chessboard to the intricate dance of the pieces, from the strategy of opening moves to the precision of endgame techniques, we've covered it all.

We've decoded the language of chess, understanding terms like 'check,' 'checkmate,' and 'stalemate.' We have also journeyed into the heart of chess strategies, exploring how to effectively control the center, launch successful attacks, and employ deft defenses. We've discovered how every piece, from the humble pawn to the mighty queen, has a unique role to play and the power to alter the course of the game.

The beauty of chess lies in its blend of simplicity and complexity, of strategy and creativity. It's a game that invites you to think, to plan, to envision and to adapt. It teaches patience, fosters resilience, and nurtures strategic thinking.

As you move forward, remember that every game of chess, whether you win or lose, is an opportunity to learn. So, keep playing, keep experimenting and keep exploring the infinite possibilities that the 64 squares hold. Whether you're aiming to be a grandmaster or simply enjoy the game, remember - in chess, as in life, the journey is as rewarding as the destination.

Happy playing, and remember: the game of chess is a treasure trove of lessons, surprises, and endless enjoyment. Your adventure has only just begun!

Don't forget to scan the QR Code to get all bonus content!

Made in the USA
Las Vegas, NV
13 November 2023

80780342R00052